DATE DUE

UPSTAIRS &
DOWNSTAIRS

THE ILLUSTRATED GUIDE TO THE REAL WORLD OF DOWNTON ABBEY

Sarah Warwick

Servants, be obedient to them that are your masters according to the flesh, with fear and trembling in singleness of your heart as unto Christ;

EPH. VI.5

CARLTON
BOOKS

This is a Carlton Book

Published in 2012 by Carlton Books Ltd
An imprint of the Carlton Publishing Group
20 Mortimer Street
London W1T 3JW

First Published in 2011 by Carlton Books Ltd

Text and design © Carlton Books Ltd 2011

A CIP catalogue record for this book is available from
the British Library.

ISBN 978 1 84732 790 1

Printed in Dubai

Contents

Introduction

The Edwardian country house was a place of extreme luxury and abject drudgery, mirroring the structure of a society that was more unequal then than at any time before or since.

Although the absolute Victorian class system had given way to a pseudo-meritocracy and it was easier for people to move up in the social ranks provided they had money, there was still a sizable chasm between rich and poor. In the household, it remained as important – if not more important than ever – for the hierarchy of the household to be strict, to reinforce the authority of those upstairs.

Many of those who owned the big houses of Edwardian Britain were not dukes or earls, but industrialists and businessmen who had made their money in trade, so formal precedence and the reiteration of status – on both sides of the class divide – made sure everybody knew their place and stayed in it.

No object represented the inflexibility of the Edwardian class system more than the green baize door. Physically dividing the world of the rich above from that of the poor below, it was powerfully symbolic. The side facing the upper house was generally richly carved out of rare woods, such as teak or mahogany, while the servants' side was covered with a layer of green baize, like the fabric on a snooker table, to muffle the unappealing smells and sounds of the lower orders.

The upper classes generally spent their winters abroad, April to June in London for "the season" and then journeyed to their estates for the remainder of the summer and autumn. These months were characterized by evenings of fine dining, shooting parties, picnicking and hunts. Almost as if they knew the end of this "golden age" of leisure was nigh, the rich spent, ate and entertained on a desperate scale, enabled by a domestic-service industry that had been honed over many centuries to a fine art.

Their servants, who often felt trapped by convention and a social system without welfare, worked a lifetime of seemingly endless days, from before dawn until midnight, satisfying the every whim and wish of their masters. The master–servant relationship was such a rigid one that even those upstairs who didn't wish to overburden their servants were reliant on them for cooking, cleaning and even dressing.

The co-dependency of these two groups, living side by side and reliant on one another, was what made the country-house world succeed but, conversely, was what was to bring it to its knees.

The lavish upper-class lifestyle of the Edwardian days was an Indian summer for the country house. With the rise of the welfare system, taxation and the impact of two world wars, this world of inequality crumbled, leaving only the houses themselves as a reminder of the people who once served and were served here.

Now, almost a century after the curtain fell on the Edwardian country house, there is a curiosity about what this life was like. Not just for the rich, who lived so lavishly, but for those below stairs. Although it is impossible to know how exactly each person lived, we have enough records and diaries of those days to be able to piece together a picture of a typical day.

Previous page *Maids such as these were to find their lives and roles expanding beyond recognition with the changes of the 20th century.*

Left *An Edwardian couple, secure – for the time being – in the highly regulated pattern of their lives.*

Before Dawn

Life in an elegant Edwardian house typically began well before daybreak, sometimes from as early as 4 am. Before any breakfast was made, many duties were carried out by the hard-working "downstairs" staff: the men and women of the "upstairs" household expected to awake to a clean and fully functioning home.

Lie-ins were bestowed only on those of highest status and getting up late was the preserve of those
born to an easy life. By contrast, servants would have to
get up before dawn, bring their masters tea in bed and
empty their "slops" (chamber pots), before preparing
breakfast and beginning a day of chores that continued
until the servants fell exhausted into bed late at night.

The lowest members of staff would be first to rise.
An early alarm at 5.30 am would wake the scullery
maid, also known as a "slavey" or "skivvy", in her attic.
After a wash with cold water from a jug (which in winter
would be thick with ice), the maid would struggle into
her corsets and uniform, pull her hair back neatly under
a cap, then go quietly down the servants' back staircase
to her duties in the kitchen.

Her first task every day was to clean the enormous
iron range. She had to scrub the stove using black lead
and lots of elbow grease, then stoke it to get the fire
going to boil water for tea. As maid of all the lowest
kitchen work, it was the scullery maid's responsibility
to make sure the range didn't go out. Ranges were very
difficult to light so they were had to be constantly fed.
They were also only about 3 per cent efficient, so most
of the coal – over 50 kg (100 lb) – shovelled into them
daily did little but fill the kitchen with heat and smoke.

While the maid was making the tea, the hall boy, the
lowliest male in the house, would get out of his pull-out
bed or mattress in the great hall, throw on his clothes
and begin his work. First on the agenda would be
"blacking" pair after pair of the household shoes, ready
to put them outside the right rooms before breakfast.
Each pair had to be faultless, polished to a high shine
and with fresh laces applied regularly. The boy would
often even have to make his own polish, from soot and
wax or old lamp oil.

As the kettle began to sing on the range, the
chambermaid would make tea. If necessary, the hall
boy would then go and wake his direct superiors, the

Previous page *The
servants of Kingston Hall in
Nottinghamshire in 1910.*

Left *A servant begins her
morning routine in 1919 by
stoking the fuel-fired stove.*

footmen, while the scullery maid would rouse the kitchen maids and housemaids.

Manservants and maidservants were kept separated from each other to prevent any promiscuity. While the girls (under the cook and housekeeper) were responsible for everyday cooking and cleaning duties, the boys, led by the butler, had more ceremonial roles and did the heavy work. Female staff slept in maids' quarters upstairs in the attics – known as "the virgins' corridor" – while the men had rooms in the basement near the kitchens. In some houses, no contact at all would have been allowed between male and female lower staff.

After the housemaids were washed and dressed, their first job was to take tea and toast up to the senior female servants (housekeeper, cook and lady's maid), while the butler would receive a tea tray from one of the footmen. The lowest-ranking male, usually the hall boy or a junior footman, would then have collected and taken out the senior servants' slops.

When all the servants had been roused, the work began in earnest. By 7 am the cook and her numerous kitchen maids would begin preparing breakfast for the household, while the scullery maid scrubbed the floors in the basement and the housemaids started work on the ground floor.

All the household cleaning, except the bedrooms, had to be done before the family came down for breakfast, so this was a daily race against time. It encompassed all the main rooms upstairs, including the study, dining rooms and drawing rooms, which had to be cleaned and tidied.

Shutters were thrown wide and all windows had to be opened briefly to air stuffy, smoky rooms. Most houses would have had electric light but few had vacuum cleaners or other electric appliances so the carpets were laboriously cleaned with a stiff brush or carpet sweeper, often after being scattered with tea leaves to mask bad odours. Ballrooms, halls and dining rooms must have seemed acres wide to the young housemaid tasked with mopping their floors.

Each housemaid had her own jobs and duties which never varied and were never shared, except when one of them was ill. The main job of the most junior housemaid was fire-lighting. Even in the height of summer, big houses were draughty, so fires had to be laid and lit in every room. After brushing out the old soot and ash, the housemaid would have to fetch kindling, coal

and wood, and lay a new fire. If she was lucky, the hall boy would have put coal and wood in the small "housemaids' cupboard" on each floor for her the night before. If she wasn't, she would have to lug scuttle after scuttle full of coal and kindling up several flights of stairs from the outhouses.

Housemaids disliked fire-lighting for two reasons: it was time consuming, as fires had to be checked every hour, and it was dirty. Although the maid would have had a dark dress and apron for the task, coal dust got everywhere and her hands soon became filthy with ingrained soot.

Dirty jobs like these were made worse by the fact that most servants were allowed only one bath a week. As they were not allowed to use the bathrooms, this meant carrying jugs of the hot water up to tin hip baths in their attic rooms and, afterwards, bringing the dirty water down the same way.

Returning to the servants' quarters after their cleaning duties, the housemaids would have found the kitchen full of activity, with the scullery maid busying cleaning floors, cook preparing breakfast for the family, the kitchen maids assisting or making porridge for the servants, and the upper servants putting together breakfast trays for their masters.

At just before 8 am, the butler would wake the gentleman of the house, bringing him the morning paper and any correspondence, as well as a choice of India or China tea, or perhaps coffee, on a tray. Unless the master had his own valet, the butler also took on dressing duties, laying out and brushing his morning clothes, running his bath and shaving him with a cut-throat razor.

Meanwhile, the lady of the house would be roused by her lady's maid, who would bring tea and toast or biscuits and any mail or messages, and would draw her mistress a bath. Other family members would usually be woken by a housemaid or footman, depending on their gender, and young children by their nursemaid.

Guests staying in the house – if they hadn't brought their own servants – would have to be served by the household staff, too. However it was usual for a well-born visitor to travel with a personal servant – valet or lady's maid – who would be billeted in the servants' quarters and live as one of the household servants for the period of their stay.

Left *Another job for a housemaid was the polishing of the furniture in the house. Depending on the size of the house, this could take a considerable amount of time.*

Below left *An illustration showing the typical clothing worn by a footman in 1902.*

Below *A young servant girl begins her working day by ironing in 1900.*

Below stairs

Status was just as important among servants as between servant and master, and the servants would have had a strict pecking order. The higher servants, known as the "Upper Ten" – including the butler, housekeeper, cook, valet and lady's maid – were in charge of the lesser ones, the "Lower Five".

Butler

Age: usually over 30; wage: £70–80* a year
Uniform: tailcoat, shirt with white wing collar, black bow-tie

Other than in the odd, very wealthy, household where an all-powerful steward was employed, the butler was the head of the servants and was responsible for ensuring the smooth day-to-day running of things below stairs. Reporting to his master, he governed the other servants with a rod of iron, looked after the downstairs accounts and managed relations between upstairs and down.

Housekeeper

Age: usually over 30; wage: £50* a year
Uniform: black dress, white cap

Often an old and trusted retainer, the housekeeper had a position of great responsibility, being in charge of all female staff, of ordering supplies and of helping her mistress to make decisions about the running of the household. She oversaw the work and wellbeing of the junior servants and kept the keys to the storerooms and pantries on a "chatelaine" – a decorative hook or ring attached to her belt with a series of chains suspended from it.

Chef

Age: usually over 30; wage: £100–150* a year for a trained chef (simple cooks £50)
Uniform: whites

While some country houses relied on the simple fare of a faithful cook (usually female) for their catering, the incessant round of high-class entertaining that was the lot of the Edwardian household meant that, increasingly, experienced male chefs were employed. In the best houses, these chefs were highly trained, having studied fine cuisine in London or – even better – Paris. These gourmets could command a huge wage (more than twice that of the butler) but were expected to produce elaborate meals at least three times a day, including dinners of up to 12 courses.

Ernest King, who was valet to rich American banker
Aksel Wichfeld in the 1920s, remembered:
"The good valet is not told what is wanted for the journey, he must know. He must be prepared to dress his man for a funeral or a fancy dress ball. He must never be caught napping, he must be able to produce everything, even shoes so well polished they may be used as a mirror in an emergency!"
A valet was a companion until the end – Mrs Wichfeld's first husband Clarence Moore and his valet Charles Harrison were on the *Titanic* when it sank, and they drowned together.

Valet

Age: usually over 25; wage £40* a year
Uniform: white shirt, black tailcoat and trousers
Known as the "gentleman's gentleman", the valet was the master's personal servant and would attend to all the master's needs, including dressing, running his bath and shaving him, as well as any matters of personal business. Traditionally the valet would have helped his master with travel arrangements, bills and correspondence. Valets often served as their masters' batmen (soldiers' servants) during wartime.

Lady's maid

Age: 25–30; wage: £30–35* a year
Uniform: her mistress's hand-me-downs, no apron
A skilled hairdresser, beautician and seamstress with a keen eye for fashion, the lady's maid was constantly at the beck and call of her mistress for outfit changes as well as clothing alterations, laundry and other personal tasks. She would accompany her mistress on any long visits to other houses, trips abroad and to London for the season.

Footmen

Age: 18+, usually in 20s; wage: dependent on experience and height, £20–35* a year
Uniform: smart livery; hair powdered for special occasions
A largely ceremonial role, footmen were the "peacocks" of the staff, hired to impress. Waiting tables, answering the door or simply standing to attention, their smart livery uniforms marked them out as status symbols. They also did some heavy work, literally lightening the maids' load by moving ice and coal, carrying heavy trays and polishing silver plate. To save their employers the bother of remembering their real names, footmen were often known as Charles or James.

Nursemaid / nanny

Age: over 18; wage: dependent on experience, about £30* a year
Uniform: white blouse and long skirt
The nanny was a position of great power within "her" nurseries. She was often in sole charge of the children of the house, who saw their parents little. She rarely left the nurseries, eating her meals upstairs instead of in the servants' hall. Many were retained in a family for years, even staying on to care for the next generation of little ones.

Housemaids

Age: late teens–20s; wage: about £20* a year
Uniform: working dress, cap and apron in morning, black dress, apron and white cap in the afternoon
When it came to cleaning, the housemaids did it all except in the kitchen: the sweeping, dusting, rug-beating, fire-laying, bed-making, bathroom-cleaning and room-tidying. After cleaning the downstairs areas and bedrooms in the morning, they spent the rest of the day following their employers and guests from room to room, tidying and picking up after them, before preparing their bedrooms for sleep.

Kitchen maids

Age: late teens; wage: about £20* a year
Uniform: cotton dress, cap and apron
These girls were under the direct command of the cook and spent their days chopping vegetables and making sauces. In houses where the cook was kept busy making the food for upstairs, the head kitchen maid would have been responsible for catering for the servants, too. In some houses, in addition to normal kitchen maids there were still-room maids, who spent their days in the still room (a small distillery), making drinks and conserves.

Laundry maid

Age: late teens; wage: £20–24* a year
Uniform: dress, apron and cap
With her whole job dedicated to washing the clothes and linens of the household, the laundry maid's life was one of repetitious drudgery. All items had to be washed, and all whites bleached, before being mangled, starched, ironed, sorted, labelled, folded and put away.

Hall boy

Age: 14–20; wage: up to £16* a year
Uniform: dark trousers, rough shirt, braces and boots
Bearing the brunt of much of the dirty work in the house was the hall boy, who cleaned and polished the household boots, sharpened knives and lugged coal and wood around for fires. Everyone except the scullery maid was his better, and any of them could give him odd jobs. He often slept in the hall, as a security measure, hence his title.

Scullery maids

Age: 14–17; wage: £12* a year
Uniform: rough cotton dress, apron, cap
Largely confined to the small room off the kitchen known as the scullery, the scullery maid's lot was not a happy one. Her chief duties were menial kitchen tasks, and she would have spent up to 18 hours a day washing pots, peeling vegetables and scrubbing the kitchen and larder floors. She was first up in the morning and had to ensure the kitchen range was clean and always kept alight.

* All wages listed are approximate.

A CHILD'S FRIENDS: BEATRIX POTTER

Beatrix Potter, like many children born into rich Victorian families, had little contact with her parents and was brought up by a succession of nursemaids and nannies.

Born Helen Beatrix Potter in London in July 1866, the author was the older child and only daughter of Rupert William and Helen Potter. Her father came from wealthy stock and, although a trained barrister, spent most of his days in leisure at gentlemen's clubs, while her mother, who had also inherited a fortune from her cotton merchant father, was a well-known socialite.

The Potter children, as was typical, would have been cared for by nursemaids or nannies in the nursery – not just "seen and not heard", but practically invisible. Most children only saw their parents once a day, for "children's hour", when they would be dressed in clean outfits and on their best behaviour.

At the time of the 1871 census, when Beatrix was four, there were five servants living with the family – Mr Louch the butler, Mrs Lowe the cook, two housemaids, Sarah and Jane, and Beatrix's nurse, Ann Mackenzie. It was during these early years that Beatrix became an animal lover and her first pet – a mouse called Hunca Munca – was said to have been found and given to her by the family butler.

She was an isolated child, and her only friend was her brother (Walter) Bertram, who was five years her junior. While Bertram was sent away to school at the age of eight, Beatrix was taught to read and write at home in Kensington by a succession of governesses.

The first of these, a Miss Hammond, encouraged Beatrix's love of animals and soon the young girl had quite a menagerie with frogs, newts, ferrets and even a pet bat. She also had two rabbits, called Peter and Benjamin, who later were to be immortalized in her stories. She took Peter everywhere, even walking him on a lead, and spent her evenings sketching him and her other animals.

When she was 16 years old, her parents engaged her last governess, a 19-year-old girl called Annie Carter, to help Beatrix learn German. The two girls remained friends even when Annie left service to marry civil engineer Edwin Moore.

Left *Beatrix Potter, aged 15.*

Above *The staircase and landing of Beatrix Potter's house, Hill Top, in the 1940s. Potter frequently used the house as inspiration for her stories.*

Right *Beatrix Potter poses outside her house in the Lake District. After her death Potter left Hill Top and its contents to the National Trust. She wanted it to be opened to the public, with all her possessions remaining in situ.*

Annie was to be the key to Beatrix's success as a children's author, both in her unstinting support and encouragement of Beatrix's writing and in supplying her with muses and willing ears for her stories. When Annie's five-year-old son, Noël, was ill with rheumatic fever in 1893 Beatrix sent a letter containing the illustrated "Tale of Peter Rabbit and Mr McGregor's Garden" to cheer him up. She continued to write stories for the Moore children over the next few years, many of which became her much-loved books.

At Christmas 1901, in the same month that "The Tailor of Gloucester" was a gift for Annie's daughter Freda, Beatrix, encouraged by the Moores, privately published the first 250 copies of *Peter Rabbit*. These cost a shilling each and were sold out within two weeks. By June 1902 there were 30,000 copies in existence and the book has never been out of print since.

Although she gave up writing in the 1920s because of failing eyesight, Beatrix remained in contact with her good friend and ex-servant Annie Carter Moore for the rest of their lives.

Above *An early edition of Potter's most famous book,* The Tale of Peter Rabbit.

Left *Potter's books remained popular even after she stopped writing them, as this edition from published in 1925 shows.*

Right *Hill Top has been accessible to the public for over 60 years. Each room features something from Beatrix's books.*

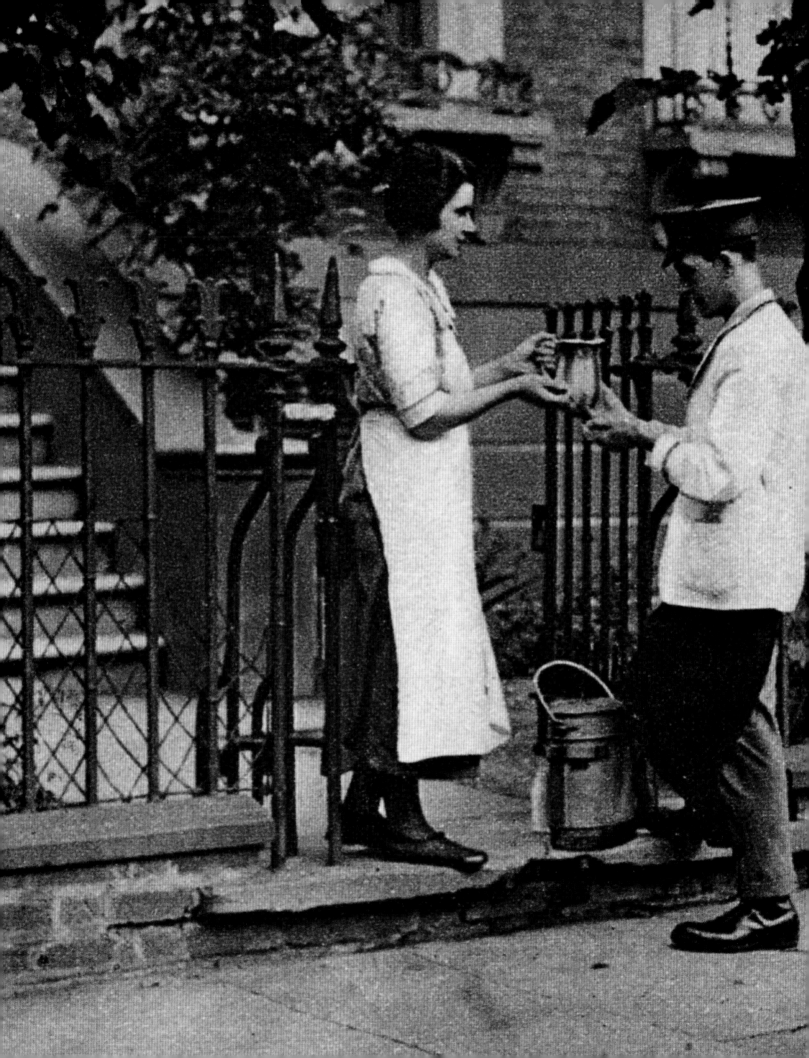

Breakfast Time

F or the servants, breakfast was a simple, filling meal before helping the master, mistress and other household members to dress and serving their repast. The breakfast served upstairs was more extravagant, usually consisting of three courses. Good table manners were expected both upstairs and downstairs.

LONDON'S SAFEST MILK

Servants knew their place and that place was in the basement, where the menservants lived and where they all had their meals and spent their limited spare time. The servants' hall, generally an unadorned room with a long table and a large window, was the centre of their world.

It was here that, already tired from up to two and a half hours of toil, the servants sat down to their breakfast at about 8 am every morning. The group assembled would have probably included various chauffeurs, grooms, gardeners and groundsmen who lived in outbuildings but ate their meals in the house. The cook or head kitchen maid – whoever was responsible for cooking most of the servants' meals – would have prepared a plain but filling meal of tea, toast and porridge, which was generally eaten in silence.

Young servants would be expected to behave impeccably during mealtimes, particularly in the presence of the butler and housekeeper. These senior servants would have been lord and mistress of the lower orders. The butler would sit at one end of the table and the housekeeper at the other, with the male servants descending in status order down the table on the butler's right side, the female servants to the butler's left. Anyone wanting to leave the table for any reason would have to ask the butler's permission.

As soon as the servants' breakfast was finished, the lady's maid would have rushed back up the back stairs to tend to her mistress, helping her to dress and doing her hair. She would have had to do this up to six times a day because in the *belle époque* ("beautiful era") – as the Edwardian years were known – ladies were expected to look impeccable, fashionable and glamorous at every hour of the day, and it took no less than four hours every day to ensure they did.

Ladies had to have clothes for every occasion: breakfast gowns, lunch frocks, tea dresses and dinner finery, plus riding and hunting outfits, clothes for sporting activity, ensembles for going to the races and demure Sunday clothes for churchgoing. The lady's maid was responsible for caring for all of these: choosing them, laying them out and washing, pressing and mending them, too.

Although a lady's maid was an essential status symbol, her presence was not just for show, as dressing was no easy task for the Edwardian lady. Every woman of the time would have worn corsets; these were shaped with whale bone and laced up with metal hooks and stays that had to be yanked tight. Although these S-shaped corsets were slightly more comfortable than their Victorian counterparts (they supported the spine and stomach, unlike the bone-crushing hourglass-shape of the 19th century), they were still confining.

The early 20th-century belief that a lot of underwear was hygienic meant that many layers of underwear were added, too. Silk stockings were attached to the corset with suspenders and long, crotchless cotton underwear would be worn underneath. Then layers of lace-trimmed

Previous page *A maid greets the local milkman in North London.*

Above *One of the greatest worries for the lady of the house was the loss of a good cook. This illustration from 1901 by Arthur Hopkins shows a cook giving her employer the news that she is leaving.*

Right *A maid prepares breakfast for her employer.*

Each to his own domain

As every type of food had its proper place below stairs, each person in the house had their place, too. The lord would have had his own study or library that others would have had to ask to enter. His wife, as well as her bedroom and dressing room (or "boudoir") upstairs, would have had a study or parlour for receiving visitors. Children had their own suite of rooms, including bedroom, nursery, playroom and schoolroom.

The senior servants below stairs also had their own domains. The butler kept his office and books in the butler's pantry. The housekeeper had her parlour, also irreverently called the "Pug's Parlour", where she did the body of her management work. Upper servants were known as pugs for their "upturned noses and downturned mouths", and this room was where they would retire after their main meal for pudding or in the evening to play cards or talk.

Just as servants weren't allowed to venture into the upstairs rooms, except to clean them, employers never ventured downstairs – except for on very special occasions. The children of the house might spend time in the servants' hall, but too much fraternizing would be frowned on by their parents.

For lower servants, their lives revolved around their places of work. Scullery maids spent most of their days in the scullery, still-room maids in the still room and the hall boy slept in the hall. They were allowed little privacy, and even the rooms that were theoretically their own – their bedrooms – were shared with several other servants. These could be searched by the housekeeper or butler on the slightest pretext.

In an echo of earlier times, the lowest servants might not even have a room of their own but might sleep on a straw mattress on the floor. Those that did have a bedroom might have on the walls of their meagrely furnished rooms framed samplers that reminded servant to know their place, for example "Humility is a servant's true dignity" or "Who sweeps a room for Thy laws makes them and their action fine".

VOTES FOR SERVANTS: EMMELINE PANKHURST

Mrs Pankhurst's suffrage campaign was given a certain sense of irony through her reliance upon – and even exploitation of – her disenfranchised servants. Domestic service in Britain was overwhelmingly female in the late 19th and early 20th centuries and, as an upper middle-class woman, Pankhurst employed several poorly paid female servants to cook, clean and care for her children. Without their aid, perhaps she would not have had the time or energy to devote to the suffrage movement.

Born Emmeline Goulden in 1858, Mrs Pankhurst grew up in Lancashire, the oldest daughter in a family of ten children. She would have been used to servants, as the family kept two maids of all work, but it wasn't until she married her husband, Richard Pankhurst, in 1878, that she was mistress of her own. At the time of the 1881 census, when Emmeline was 22, she had two servants: a cook, Katherine Kneole, aged 18, and housemaid Amelia Kneole, 16, presumably sisters.

At this time Emmeline had only one child, Christabel, but by the next census in 1891 she was mother to four (a fifth having

Right *The children of Emmeline Pankhurst: Sylvia, Adela and Christabel.*

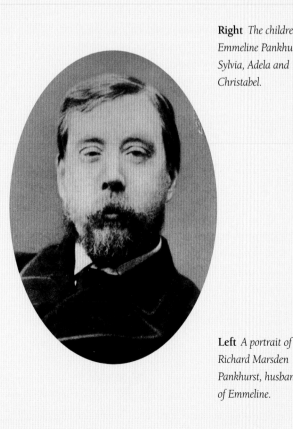

Left *A portrait of Richard Marsden Pankhurst, husband of Emmeline.*

died young) and her household included a cook and housemaid as before, as well as a nursemaid for the children. This long-standing nanny was Susannah Jones, who was first engaged after the second Pankhurst daughter, Sylvia, was born in 1882.

Nanny was to play a key role in the lives of Emmeline's daughters. In their accounts of their childhoods, written much later, they recalled how busy and absent their mother was, and how they were often left with Susannah and the servants while their mother travelled. From nanny they received a lack of warmth, and some stern discipline. Sylvia even remembered being tied to the bed when she wouldn't drink her cod liver oil.

Whatever her children thought of their upbringing, for Emmeline a reliance on staff meant the freedom to pursue a

political career. Several trips to America, plus activity in local government followed. Her activities were only briefly curtailed by the death of her husband in 1898, which forced her to take up paid employment as a registrar. Even though she wasn't paid much for this, it was still enough to retain two servants to do her cooking and cleaning.

By this point Emmeline's daughters had grown and they – particularly Christabel and Sylvia – joined her in the fight for women's rights as members of the Women's Social and Political Union (WSPU). As the WSPU struggle intensified, the Pankhursts moved to London, taking up a house in Russell Square. Alongside their sister suffragettes, they committed desperate acts of vandalism, arson and trespass – Emmeline was imprisoned 14 times – but ultimately secured all women the vote.

For the servants who had shouldered the burden of her household throughout her struggle, surely this was the greatest reward? Emmeline's daughter Adela summed up her own gratitude in a biography of her mother, saying, "What we lost as a mother, we gained as a political figure." (*My Mother: An Explanation and a Vindication*, 1933)

Above *This cartoon from the early 20th century mocks the suffragette campaign that Emmeline Pankhurst devoted her life to.*

Lunchtime

Traditionally, lunch had been the main meal of the day. By Edwardian times, however, customs had changed, and a comparatively light meal was usually served, although it was still three courses for those living upstairs. Lunch for the servants of the house was a hastier, if vital, deal.

Left *The most important lunch party of the Second World War, 29 August 1941. Representatives of the Allied governments sit upstairs at the Soviet Embassy in London. Winston Churchill is at centre right.*

Above left *Two women "walk" their bikes on a station platform.*

Right *Watching a game from the terrace of an English country house.*

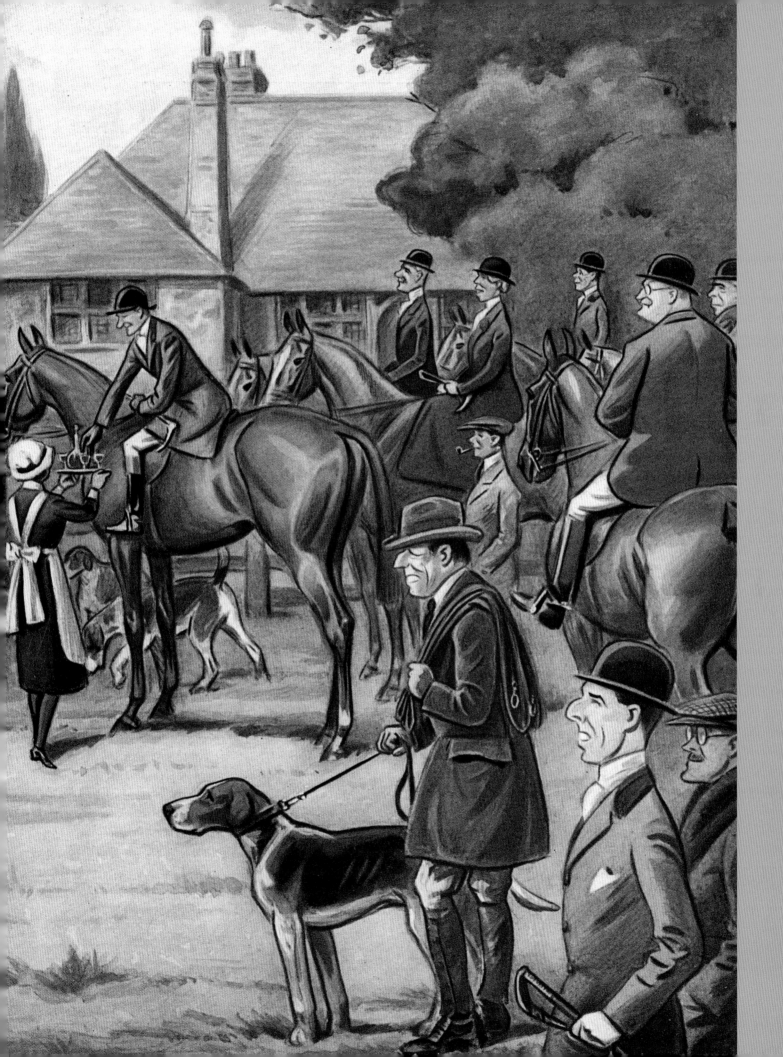

The cost of shooting, which soared in the 1910s, was one of the main gripes of the upper classes. The Earl of Crawford complained in his journal for 6–10 August 1913:
"The equipment, the paraphernalia and above all the cost of grouse-driving increases every year. The wages of the drivers, mostly boys from the local villages, have largely increased and one now pays five shillings a day to these youths; and into the bargain they have to be driven to the moor... but when the last increase in wages was conceded, their free lunch was knocked off, which is considered a real advantage as the boys now bring their own frugal bread and cheese with them whereas they previously gorged themselves at their employer's expense so freely as to find post-prandial walking a hard and uninviting task."

Above *A footman serves his master wine at a hunt in 1923.*

Left *A gentleman instructs a lady in a country garden on the best way to play bowls.*

Left *Salmon-fishing in the river. Part of the groundskeeper's job was to keep lakes and rivers on their estate well stocked.*

Previous pages *A wealthy group of men at a hunting party in 1910.*

tailored clothing, and – as the Edwardian period continued to progress – these fashions were copied by the daughters of the gentry and embraced as the ideal outfits for cycling and riding, tennis or golf.

Despite this fledgling feminism, the countryside still enjoyed traditional pursuits. Riding to hounds, or hunting, was the most popular pastime enjoyed by both sexes, with 350 hunts around the country. During the early days of the 20th century, hunting was so popular that foxes had to be imported from Europe to keep up with demand. The local hunt would often be sponsored by the landowner and would begin on his estate, with all members having a glass of port or beer, provided by the footmen, before setting off.

Fishing was another popular pastime. The master – or rather, his groundskeeper – would make sure the lakes and rivers on the estate were always well stocked with salmon and trout, so he could invite persons of eminence to join him in a spot of angling. Shooting (see page 80) completed the holy trinity of outdoor pursuits.

In all of these activities – as in every aspect of their pampered existences – Edwardians followed the lead of their king. His influence could be seen everywhere, from hairstyles to house parties, but nowhere was it as warmly embraced as in horse-racing. In the 1900s racetracks were the closest thing Britain had to a place of equality. Race meets at Ascot and Epsom were the

Left *A young couple watching swans pass by on the river as they enjoy a country picnic.*

Above *A gardener holds tomatoes in his apron, fresh for the family's evening meal.*

height of sophistication, but even a servant on his half-day off might have visited the course for a flutter.

Mimicking the king, many of the gentry invested in racehorses – a thoroughbred was seen as one of the essential accessories for the upper-class male – and went to watch them triumph. Depending on how wealthy they were, they might also copy the king's other investments, in yachting and, even those without boats of their own made excursions to the social events of the Cowes summer yachting festival on the Isle of Wight.

For the servants, afternoons were less frenetic than the mornings. They might even have the opportunity of some rest time. Each servant would have one half-day a week off, and the rest of the staff, providing they'd finished their work, would get a break from 2 pm until 4 o'clock to sit and chat with the other servants, or do some quiet household mending.

In practice, however, the work was rarely finished, especially when there were guests staying in the house, their bells ringing for attention at any hour of the day, or a dinner party to prepare for. The housekeeper and cook would have been hard at work preparing for dinner and afternoon tea, while in the gardens the groundsmen would be digging, weeding and picking fruit and flowers for the house. Every time the mistress and her guests changed their clothes, maids would have to tidy their bedrooms again, and fires had to be tended to ensure that they were kept burning when the rooms' inhabitants returned.

Even when servants did have some free time, there wasn't much that they could do with it. They couldn't invite their friends and relatives to visit them, and – unlike their counterparts in London who could meet friends and go to the pictures or a Lyons tea room – there wasn't much within walking distance except the local village.

The family and their guests would take high tea at about 5 pm. This might be as simple as a cup of tea in fine china tea cups and a piece of cake, but could be a complex spread of finger sandwiches, cakes and scones. Among the favourites for teatime were cucumber, cheese or egg sandwiches; sponge cakes; scones, with clotted cream and strawberry jam; sliced cold meats; asparagus tips; cheese canapés garnished with tomatoes and pickles; salmagundi – a popular kind of pot-luck salad with meat, fish, nuts, vegetables and even flowers; home-made ice cream; flavoured jellies and biscuits. In the winter tea would be taken in the drawing room, but in the summer months it would often be served outside on a south-facing lawn by a maid in her frilly cap and apron, and was the ideal break during a lawn-tennis game or croquet match.

HALF-DAY OFF

In 1914, 15-year-old Annie Norman was a maid in Repton in the Midlands. She kept a diary including all the things she did with her time off:

1 Feb: I went out in the afternoon with Dora on the Willington Road. I met Nellie Williams and Rene R. We then went to Mrs Perry's for tea and then went to Church with Esther Wright, then we went on another walk till 9.15.

5 Feb: I went to the Parish tea at 6 o'clock ... I had three dances and came back to "The Pastures" at 10 o'clock

15 Feb: We had morning tea at 5.15 am in bed. Emily went to church in the morning and I went to Mrs Perry's for tea with Dora and we had some games ... and then we all went to Willington for a walk and we didn't half have some fun, all five of us.

18 Feb: I went to Esther's for tea and went to visit Mr Wright and Mrs Perry. Ellen was with me and we both went to the rink dancing and came in at 10.15.

Right *Four maids work at hand-washing the family laundry with wash-pails.*

Shooting

House parties held in August were invariably known as shooting parties, as there was rarely anything else on people's minds but shooting pheasant and grouse. Every morning of a three-day shoot, the host would lead a group of men, replete after a hearty breakfast, out onto his lands to shoot.

A group of beaters, made up of the groundskeeper, outdoor staff and hired local men, would drive the birds out of bushes and shrubs into the path of the gun-toting gentry. Gun dogs would retrieve the birds from the brush. The guns would swap places at every new drive (location) so everybody got a chance to be at the prime position in the centre of the line.

The sport was embraced with enthusiasm. Vast amounts of money were spent – an estimate in *Tatler* in 1911 put the annual figure at £8,182,000 (about £500 million in today's money). That figure included daily wages for beaters (equivalent to a maid's weekly salary), double-barrelled shotguns, planting copses for the birds to live and breed in, and buying or breeding huge numbers of birds. Men wore tweed Norfolk jackets – named for the king's country estate at Sandringham in that county – which allowed their arms to be raised up in order to fire.

A prodigious number of birds was needed just to keep pace with the appetite for these weekend parties – some shoots bagged more than 1,000 birds a day. The most famous shoot of the time took place at a Buckingham estate in 1913, where a group of crack shots, including King George V, bagged close to 4,000. Although individuals might carry a counting device, known as a "Norfolk liar", for recording their own kills, a group haul was the aim of the game and it was considered vulgar to boast about individual triumphs.

At least some of the birds killed were destined for the pot. The appetite for pheasant was phenomenal and cookery books of the time reveal numerous ways of cooking it, like casseroled in port or stuffed with foie gras. Before cooking, the meat was hung in a larder for several days – even weeks – before cooking, until the meat would be considered putrid by modern tastes. Edwardian cooks believed that the decomposition added to the flavour of the meat and boiled the maggots off into the stock during the cooking process.

It wasn't just the rich who wanted pheasant on their tables and the big estates began to attract poachers. As a result, owners upped the protection of their birds to the point where the 1911 census counted twice as many gamekeepers in some rural areas as policemen.

Men who didn't shoot were few and far between, but those that didn't shoot proved popular with the "shooting widows", who were glad to have some male companionship. These men – known as "darlings" or "lapdogs" (or referred to by other men as "sporting eunuchs") – were not always as effeminate as their contemporaries liked to believe, and it wasn't unknown for affairs to begin while the rest of the men were off shooting.

BEHIND EVERY GREAT MAN: WINSTON CHURCHILL

As a busy man and a great statesman, Winston Churchill had a reputation for being brisk and impatient with his under-secretaries and servants, but as a child his greatest friend was his nanny.

Soon after he was born in 1874, a woman named Elizabeth Anne Everest was engaged to be his nursemaid. She was his main confidante, comforter and caregiver. He slept in her room; she washed, changed and fed him, and was in every respect a surrogate mother to him.

This role was vitally needed in little Winston's life, as Sir Randolph and Lady Churchill were distant even by Victorian standards. Until he was five and his brother was born, Winston and his nanny were each other's exclusive companions, and he saw his parents only once a week or so. Everest, or "Woomanny" as the future premier called her, more than made up for this: she doted on and over-indulged the boy and he adored her.

Above *A portrait of Winston Churchill as a baby.*

Above right *Winston Churchill's nanny, Elizabeth Anne Everest. He kept a photo of her by his bed all his life.*

On the 1881 census, Winston, then aged six, John, aged one, and E A Everest, "nursemaid, 44", are listed with the rest of their household: mother, father and seven other servants, including an under nursemaid.

Even after Winston was sent away to school, aged eight, the boy and his nurse kept in touch, sending letters and presents to one another. Elizabeth Everest continued to watch over him and it was she who told his mother that Winston was getting badly beaten at his first prep school, which led – to his delight – to him being removed. When Winston caught pneumonia at the age of 11, it was only her devoted nursing that saved his life. In return he worried about her when she was sick and sent his mother letters asking her to ensure that "Everest" was getting the right medical treatment.

Although she left his parents' service in 1893, when Churchill was 18, and went to live with her sister in north

Left *Winston Churchill
as a young man
wearing his uniform for
the armed services.*

Right *Churchill as
a child strikes a
confident pose.*

London, nanny continued to send him long letters, which he treasured. Then, when his father died in 1895 and he took on the family estate, Churchill began to support Mrs Everest, sending her regular sums, even though – after debts and death duties – money was tight.

In the end, though, neither his love nor money could save Nanny Everest: in late 1895 she suffered a bout of peritonitis that was to prove fatal. As soon as he heard she was ill, Churchill went to London to see her, staying until she died. He wrote later that "death came very easily to her... she lived such an innocent loving life in service of others. She had been my dearest and most intimate friend during the whole of the 20 years I had lived." (*My Early Life,* 1930)

After her death, he and his brother Jack erected a grave for her in the City of London cemetery, and he paid an annual sum for many years to a local florist to put flowers on it. He mentioned her throughout his life, always with great affection, and when he died in 1965, at the age of 90, there was only one picture by his bedside and that was of her, his darling nursemaid, Elizabeth Everest, who had died some 70 years before.

Above *The exterior of Chartwell, the home of Winston Churchill.*

Left *Father of Churchill, Lord Randolph Henry Spencer Churchill, who was also a politician.*

Above *Winston Churchill and his wife relax outside Chartwell.*

Left *Churchill's mother with her sons, John (left) and Winston (right), in 1885.*

The End of the Day

As the century drew on, World War One would soon herald an abrupt challenge to the rigorous class and gender divisions that underlay the worlds of upstairs and downstairs. For better or worse, in a few short years, both servants and leisured gentry would find their old ways of life were no longer tenable.

Although change would soon be in the air, in the meantime those ladies and gentlemen relaxing after dinner would have been blissfully unaware that their time was drawing to an end. After debating matters of worldly importance, the men would follow the ladies into the drawing room for drinks, perhaps with some gentle dancing or card-playing.

Gambling in all its forms was fashionable, including 21 (known as *Vingt-et-Un*) and the newly imported American game of Poker, but not the notorious Baccarat, which had fallen out of favour in 1895 after the king (then Prince of Wales) was implicated in a gambling scandal. If they had finished all their chores downstairs, the servants might also play cards in their hall, although they played for matchsticks, not the high stakes wagered upstairs.

As the initial devastating losses of the First World War began to bite, employers were urged to give up

their manservants for the war effort. "Have you a Butler, Groom, Chauffeur, Gardener or Gamekeeper serving you who, at this moment, should be serving your King and Country?" asked *Country Life* magazine in 1915. "Have you a man serving at your table who should be serving a gun? Have you a man digging your garden who should be digging trenches? Ask your men to enlist TODAY!"

Between the two world wars – during the time of the "bright young things", as writer Evelyn Waugh christened the hedonists of the 1920s – these after-dinner activities upstairs could go on for many hours. Waugh and his contemporaries, including the playwrights Noël Coward and Terrence Rattigan, painted a convincingly vivid picture of this decadent period, which was so full of cultural and artistic excitements that the French nicknamed it the *années folles* ("crazy years").